Centennial Hills

Scholastic First Dictionary
Activity Book

by Lorraine Hopping Egan

SCHOLASTIC
PROFESSIONAL BOOKS

New York • Toronto • London • Auckland • Sydney
Mexico City • New Delhi • Hong Kong • Buenos Aires

Dedication · · · · · · · · · · · · · ·

To Pat Horan, who is the definition of diligence and whose words of wisdom have greatly improved this book.

Cover design by Adrián Avilés
Cover illustrations by Amanda Haley
Interior design by Sydney Wright
Interior illustrations by Amanda Haley and Rusty Fletcher

ISBN: 0-439-30464-4

2 3 4 5 6 7 8 9 10   40   08 07 06 05 04 03

Contents

Introduction and Skills Chart

Here's what the games, puzzles, and activities in *Scholastic First Dictionary Activity Book* will do for your students:

◆ teach children what information is inside a dictionary.

◆ teach them how to find and use that information.

◆ entertain and motivate them to learn with jokes (Q: What do you call tight pants? A: mean jeans), riddles (What sleeps with its shoes on?), and fun games, including a board game, relay races, card games, and scavenger hunt.

Here's what this book will do for you:

◆ provide multi-level materials to accommodate a range of ability levels.

◆ supply complete game sets (spinners, cards, game boards, puzzle pieces, and reproducibles) so that you don't have to make materials from scratch.

◆ teach language arts skills along with dictionary skills; specific skill topics are listed on this page.

Skills Chart

Skill Topics	Pages
alphabetizing	5, 13, 22, 28, 29
classification	5, 11, 22
definitions and usage	5, 7, 11, 22
diagrams	7
looking up words	5, 7, 11, 13, 18, 24, 25, 26, 27, 28, 29
prefixes	18
pronunciation	5, 30, 31, 32
rhyming words	7, 13, 28, 29
spelling	5, 13, 18, 24, 25, 26, 27, 30, 31, 32
using an index	7
vocabulary	5, 7, 11, 13, 18, 22, 24, 25
word forms	5, 7

All Set! Games

Teams compete or cooperate to sort the parts of a dictionary entry—pronunciation, word forms, definition, example—into matching sets.

Preparation

Split students into teams. Make card decks (page 6) as needed. (See "Playing the Games"). Review the parts of a dictionary entry on page 5 of the *Scholastic First Dictionary*. Demonstrate how to form a four-card set.

Playing the Games

The Goal Correctly sort 32 cards into eight sets. Each set includes a pronunciation guide, word forms, definition, and sample sentence for a word.

Simple Sorting Each team needs one card deck. Team captains deal out the cards as evenly as possible. Teams must correctly sort their cards into eight sets, one for each word. Competitive: The first team to do so is the winner. Cooperative: Teams have a time limit such as 5 minutes. Ask each team to read aloud a set.

Relay Race Teams will create a chart (see next page) by posting cards on the board. Make one deck of enlarged cards with adhesive such as Tac™ on the backs. Write the eight words across the top of the board. List the categories (pronunciation, word forms, definition, sentence) down the left side. Deal the cards evenly to teams. Post any leftover cards in place on the board. Teams take turns posting one card per turn. If a racer makes a mistake, the team waits until its next turn to try again. The winner is the first team to post all its cards.

Mystery Game Cover some of the entries on the chart (page 6) before copying it. Ask partners to fill in the missing information, using the *Scholastic First Dictionary* as reference.

Concentration Each group of 2 to 6 players needs a card deck. Put cards facedown in a grid. Players take turns flipping over any two cards. If the two cards that belong to the same word, players keep the match. If not, they put the cards back in place. When all 32 cards are gone, the winner is the player with the most matches.

Pass the Card Three to eight students need a deck that has only as many words as there are players (e.g., for four players use only four words—half the deck). The dealer deals out all the cards. Each player should have four cards. Players can look at their cards but should use their arm to hide them from others. The goal is to collect a four-card set. At the same time, each player passes a card to the right. Then, quickly, everyone passes another card. The faster, the better. Players keep passing until a winner has a four-card set and says, "All set!"

Variations Substitute or add your own cards to the deck. All Set! is great for practicing spelling or vocabulary words.

Once students have completed sets, ask them to alphabetize the words or write an original sample sentence for each one.

pronunciation	word forms	definition	sentence example
add **(ad)**	**adding, added**	To **add** means to put something together with something else.	If you **add** 2 and 3, you get 5.
far **(far)**	**farther, farthest**	1. **Far** means away from or not close.	It is too **far** for Michele to walk to my house.
giggle **(gig-**uhl**)**	**giggling, giggled**	When you **giggle**, you laugh with short, quick sounds.	At the movie, all of the kids were **giggling**.
good **(gud)**	**better, best**	2. **Good** means that you do something well.	Daryl is a **good** skater, but Karla is a better one.
hero **(hir-**oh**) and** **heroine** **(her-**uh-wuhn**)**	**heroes, heroines**	A **hero** helps and protects other people.	The mayor thanked the **heroes** and **heroines** who helped people.
keep **(keep)**	**keeping, kept**	3. To **keep** means to stop from going somewhere or doing something.	The fence **keeps** the dog in the yard.
powder **(poud-**uhr**)**	**powders**	A **powder** is made of very tiny pieces of something dry.	Mom puts **powder** all over the baby's body after his bath.
silly **(sil-**ee**)**	**sillier, silliest**	If something is **silly**, it is funny and not serious.	Carmen drew a very **silly** picture of a giraffe dancing.

Peek and Seek Races ···· ▪ ▫ ▽ ▪

In these word rallies, teams race to locate items in the Scholastic First Dictionary. Need a quick time filler? Keep the dictionary and the list of items handy and challenge students to find an item or two between other activities.

▷ Preparation

Pass out one copy per team of a Peek and Seek form (pages 8–10). Each team needs a *Scholastic First Dictionary*. Not enough dictionaries? Make an overhead transparency of a form and complete it as a class.

▷ Playing the Games

The Goal "Peek" in the dictionary and "seek" out a picture or a word. All items are located in the *Scholastic First Dictionary*. The winner is first team to find the most items within a time limit.

Peek and Seek Race 1: Pictures asks questions about the pictures in the dictionary. Discuss the "Using Your Dictionary" section on page 4 of the dictionary. Point out the picture of the snakes and the labels, in particular. Ask students to locate the same page in the dictionary (page 172).

Peek and Seek Race 2: Words gives students practice in looking up words and reading and understanding definitions. Before playing, look up a few words using the alphabet bars on the edges of the pages and the guide words.

Peek and Seek Race 3: Scavenger Hunt encompasses both pictures and entries. Students also use the picture index (page 223).

Fast and Easy Variation Ask students to find an interesting word or picture in the dictionary and share their findings with the class.

▷ Answers ··

Peek and Seek Race 1: Pictures
1. hose, flippers, or boots (other answers possible) 2. orange, red, or yellow 3. ice cream, milk, cheese, yogurt 4. chimpanzee 5. red, white, green

Peek and Seek Race 2: Words
1. angry 2. yellow and blue 3. balloon or egg (other answers are possible) 4. smile 5. libraries

Peek and Seek Race 3: Scavenger Hunt
1. heroes 2. salad items are pictured on page 157 (other answers are possible) 3. underwater
4. 8 ounces (also see page 222) 5. eating, ate, eaten

Peek and Seek Race 1: Pictures

**Look up each word in dark letters
in the *Scholastic First Dictionary*.
Look at the picture near the word.
Answer the question.**

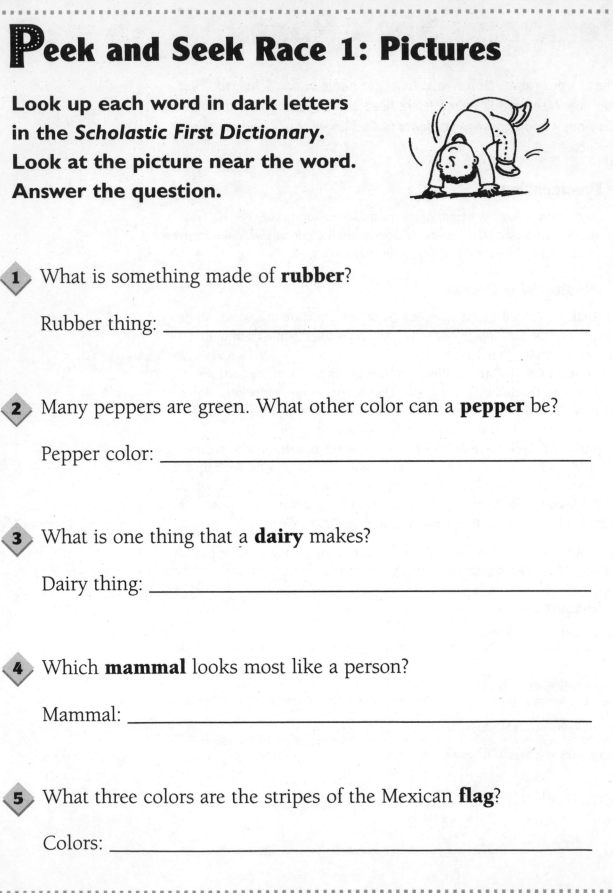

1 What is something made of **rubber**?

Rubber thing: _____

2 Many peppers are green. What other color can a **pepper** be?

Pepper color: _____

3 What is one thing that a **dairy** makes?

Dairy thing: _____

4 Which **mammal** looks most like a person?

Mammal: _____

5 What three colors are the stripes of the Mexican **flag**?

Colors: _____

Peek and Seek Race 2: Words

Look up each word in dark letters in the *Scholastic First Dictionary*. Read about the word. Answer the question.

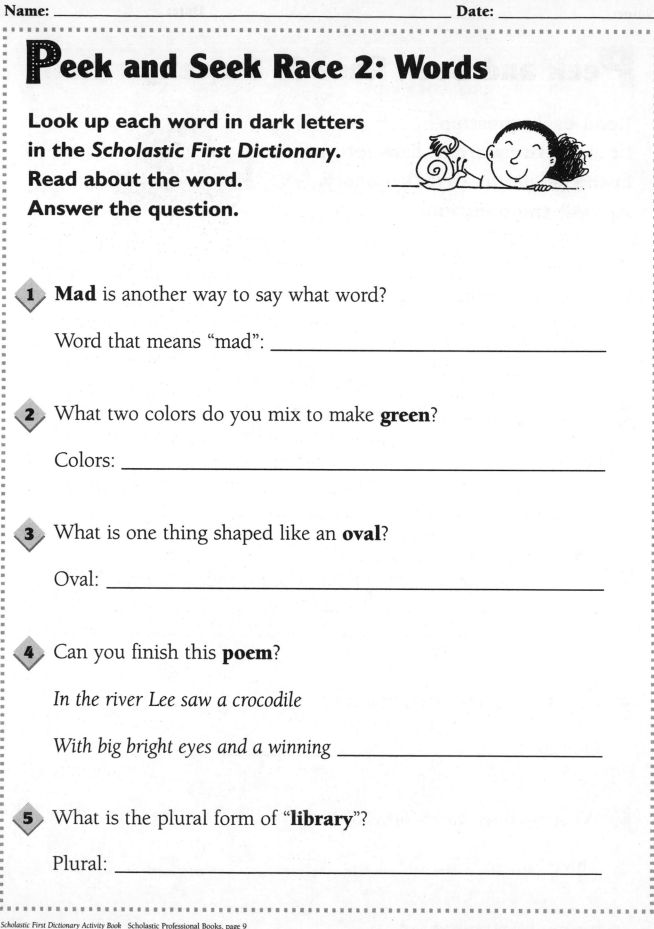

1 **Mad** is another way to say what word?

Word that means "mad": _____

2 What two colors do you mix to make **green**?

Colors: _____

3 What is one thing shaped like an **oval**?

Oval: _____

4 Can you finish this **poem**?

In the river Lee saw a crocodile

With big bright eyes and a winning _____

5 What is the plural form of "**library**"?

Plural: _____

Peek and Seek Race 3: Scavenger Hunt

Read each question.
Look up the word in dark letters
in the *Scholastic First Dictionary*.
Answer the question.

1 What is the plural of "**hero**"?

Plural: _____

2 What are two vegetables in a **salad**?

Vegetable: _____

Vegetable: _____

3 Where do **moray eels** live? (Hint: Use the index on page 223.)

Place: _____

4 How many **ounces** are in a cup?

Ounces: _____

5 What are three word forms of "**eat**"?

Three Forms: _____

What's This? Game

Teams or partners look up the definitions of words to classify them into things you eat, wear, or use.

▷ Preparation

For each pair or team of students, make one copy of one of the What's This? reproducible on the next page.

▷ Playing the Games

The Goal Complete the form as quickly as possible; accuracy counts more than speed. Teams that finish early can use the *Scholastic First Dictionary* to locate one more item for each category.

If you have a class set of dictionaries, play an "I Spy"-like version. Call out guide words (for example, "dog to door"). Students race to find the corresponding page of the dictionary and name an item on that page that is in a certain category, either eat, wear, or use.

Variations: Challenge students to classify other words such as animals (octopus, ostrich, amphibian, reptile, and so on), places (desert, habitat, harbor, space, tunnel, factory, continent, and so on), and things in found in a house (furniture, furnace, drawer, dollhouse, and so on).

▷ Answers ···

What's This? (page 12)
What's This? 1: Eat: 1, 3, 5, 8. Wear: 2, 4, 6, 7.
What's This? 2: Eat: 3, 6, 8. Use: 1, 2, 4, 5, 7.

What's This?

Look up each word in a dictionary. Read what it means.
Then circle "eat it" or "wear it." The first one is done for you.

Game 1	**Circle one.**
1. vitamin	Do you (eat it) or **wear it** ?
2. jewelry	Do you **eat it** or **wear it** ?
3. pasta	Do you **eat it** or **wear it** ?
4. uniform	Do you **eat it** or **wear it** ?
5. raspberry	Do you **eat it** or **wear it** ?
6. sneaker	Do you **eat it** or **wear it** ?
7. costume	Do you **eat it** or **wear it** ?
8. vegetable	Do you **eat it** or **wear it** ?

Look up each word in a dictionary. Read what it means. Then
circle "use it" or "eat it." The first one is done for you.

Game 2	**Circle one.**
1. instrument	Do you **eat it** or (use it) ?
2. furniture	Do you **eat it** or **use it** ?
3. squash	Do you **eat it** or **use it** ?
4. refrigerator	Do you **eat it** or **use it** ?
5. harmonica	Do you **eat it** or **use it** ?
6. poultry	Do you **eat it** or **use it** ?
7. telescope	Do you **eat it** or **use it** ?
8. dessert	Do you **eat it** or **use it** ?

Word Factory Board Games

Two to four players race to the finish by combining letters to form words (for example, b + old = bold). There are two levels of play.

Preparation

Each playing group needs a game board (page 15 or 16), a spinner (page 14), optional cards (page 17), and playing pieces (dry pasta, dry beans, counters, buttons, or similar items). Appoint a judge to check answers in a *Scholastic First Dictionary* or on the Word List below. Hint: If possible, laminate the game board to make it sturdier.

Playing the Games

The Goal Rules for playing the game are on the board for Word Factory One. Stress: Two players never land on the same space (except for "Begin here."). Players always move forward to the next *empty* space, leapfrogging their way to the finish. The optional cards have word-related questions. Point out that all of the words end in one of the four choices on the spinner.

Variations Make spinners with other word combinations such as ace, ad, ain, air, ag, all, ame, amp, an, and, ap, ar, are, ash, ate, ead, eep, est, ew, ick, ight, ing, ill, ind, ink, it, ive, ock, og, ook, ool, orn, ot, own, ug, ump. For a smooth and swift game, make sure that each letter on the game board forms at least two words with the letter combinations on the spinner.

Word List

Word Factory One			Word Factory Two			
bail	*hail*	*sake*	bat	flat	meat	sat
bake	hear	*sear*	*bay*	*flay*	*mow*	say
bear	hold	sold	beat	flow	*nay*	seat
bold	mail	snail	*bleat*	gray	neat	*slat*
cake	make	snake	blow	great	*now*	*slay*
cold	*mold*	tail	bow	grow	*pat*	slow
fail	hail	take	cat	hat	pay	*sow*
fake	hear	tear	*cay*	hay	*peat*	stay
fear	pail	told	chat	heat	play	*stow*
flail	pear		cheat	*how*	*pleat*	tray
flake	rail		chow	lay	plow	treat
fold	rake		cow	low	*pow*	
gear	*rear*		*fat*	mat	*ray*	
gold	sail		*feat*	*may*	row	

Note: All words except those italicized are listed in the *Scholastic First Dictionary*.

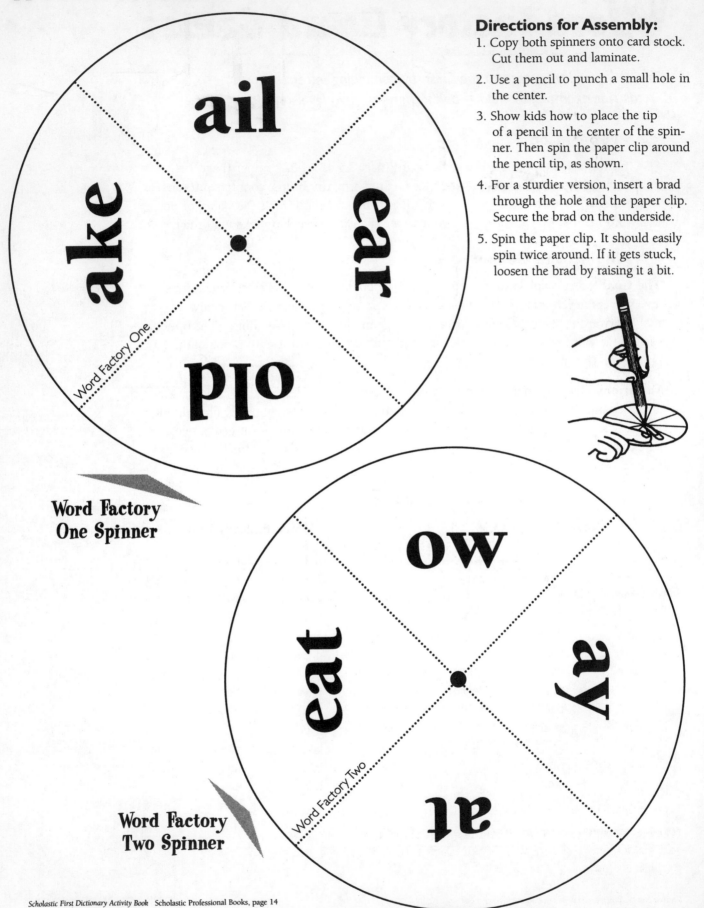

ail

ake

ear

old

Word Factory One

Word Factory One Spinner

ow

eat

ay

at

Word Factory Two

Word Factory Two Spinner

Directions for Assembly:

1. Copy both spinners onto card stock. Cut them out and laminate.

2. Use a pencil to punch a small hole in the center.

3. Show kids how to place the tip of a pencil in the center of the spinner. Then spin the paper clip around the pencil tip, as shown.

4. For a sturdier version, insert a brad through the hole and the paper clip. Secure the brad on the underside.

5. Spin the paper clip. It should easily spin twice around. If it gets stuck, loosen the brad by raising it a bit.

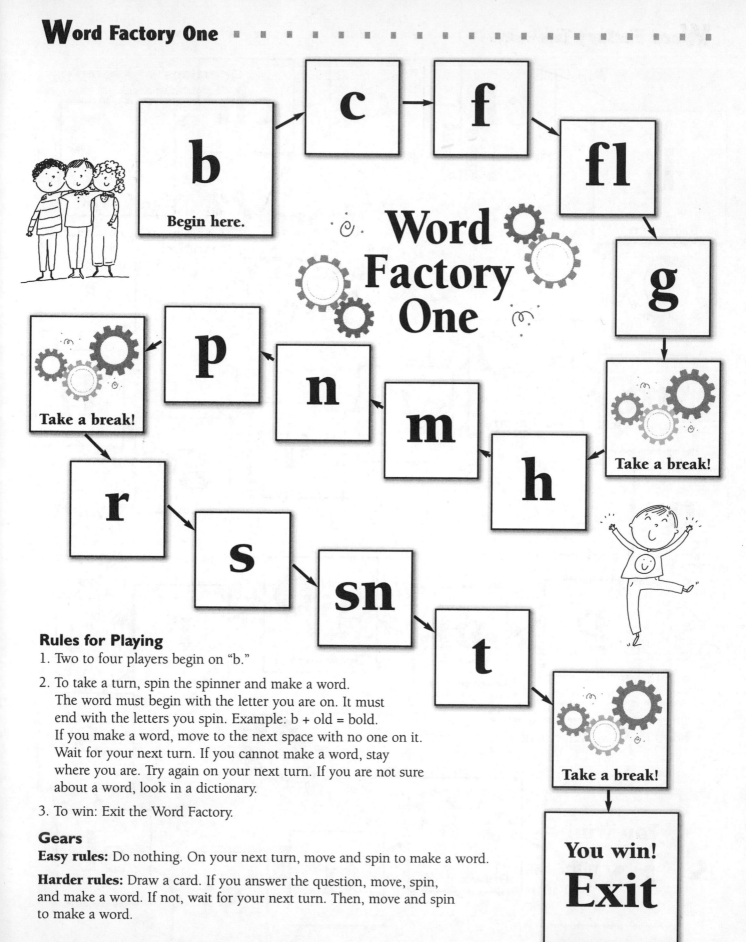

b Begin here.

c

f

fl

Word Factory One

g

Take a break!

p

n

m

h

Take a break!

r

s

sn

t

Take a break!

You win! Exit

Rules for Playing

1. Two to four players begin on "b."

2. To take a turn, spin the spinner and make a word.
   The word must begin with the letter you are on. It must
   end with the letters you spin. Example: b + old = bold.
   If you make a word, move to the next space with no one on it.
   Wait for your next turn. If you cannot make a word, stay
   where you are. Try again on your next turn. If you are not sure
   about a word, look in a dictionary.

3. To win: Exit the Word Factory.

Gears

Easy rules: Do nothing. On your next turn, move and spin to make a word.

Harder rules: Draw a card. If you answer the question, move, spin,
and make a word. If not, wait for your next turn. Then, move and spin
to make a word.

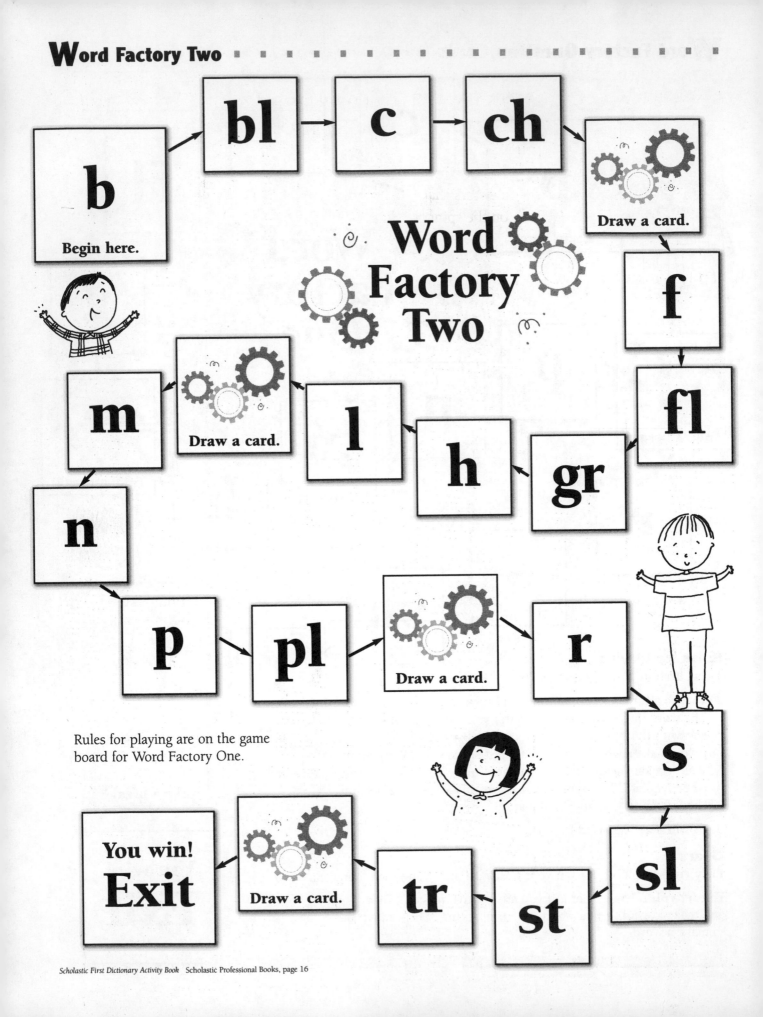

b
Begin here.

bl → **c** → **ch**

Draw a card.

Word Factory Two

f

fl

m

Draw a card.

l

h

gr

n

p → **pl**

Draw a card.

r

s

Rules for playing are on the game board for Word Factory One.

You win! **Exit**

Draw a card.

tr

st

sl

Word Factory Question Cards (Optional)

Word Factory 1 What word sounds like "deer" but is not spelled the same? d __ __ __	**Word Factory 1** What word sounds like "steak" but ends with letters that are on the spinner? st __ __ __	**Word Factory 1** When you feel the ground shake, it might be an earthqu __ __ __	**Word Factory 1** What body of water is bigger than a pond and smaller than an ocean? l __ __ __
Word Factory 1 On the spinner, which word means "not young"? __ __ __	**Word Factory 1** What word means "path" and ends with letters on the spinner? tr __ __ __	**Word Factory 1** What word sounds like "sale" but is not spelled the same? s __ __ __	**Word Factory 1** What word can join "milk" to form a new word? milksh __ __ __
Word Factory 2 What word can join "blue" to form a new word? bluej __ __	**Word Factory 2** What is a large, black bird called? cr __ __	**Word Factory 2** What word means the same as "toss"? thr __ __	**Word Factory 2** What word sounds like "grate" but is not spelled the same? gr __ __ __
Word Factory 2 What word means "TV program"? sh __ __	**Word Factory 2** What soft, squishy stuff do you use in art class? cl __ __	**Word Factory 2** Change one letter in "play" to make a new word. p __ ay	**Word Factory 2** A "prow" is the front of a ship. Change one letter to make a farm tool. p __ ow

Word Train Puzzles

Partners or individuals connect prefixes and roots to form words.

▶ Preparation

Cut out the Word Train puzzle pieces (pages 19 or 20). Hint: To help the puzzle pieces last longer, laminate them, if possible. Partners need a *Scholastic First Dictionary* and a long table; each puzzle is about 40 inches long. Review prefixes (page 219 of the dictionary).

▶ Solving the Puzzles

The Goal Put all 10 prefix-root pieces into a chain to form nine words. Students can work on their own or with a friend.

Two-Player Rules One partner starts with the locomotive and the other with the caboose. Players add pieces to their end of the train, each piece forming a word, until the pieces meet in the middle. If the middle pieces don't make a word, there's a mistake. Students must start over or rearrange pieces to fix it.

Players can look up the letters of each prefix (e.g., "dis") in the *Scholastic First Dictionary* and read the words listed (e.g., *disappear, disappoint, discover*). One of the words will match a word that's on a puzzle piece.

Word Train Game Two players turn the pieces facedown, scramble them, and each draw five pieces. Players take turns playing a piece, Dominoes-style, to form words. If a player can't play, he or she passes and waits for the next turn. The object is to run out of pieces first.

Variations Use the template (page 21) to make your own Word Trains. Using nine different prefixes cuts down on the number of possible matches, making the puzzles easier to solve. It also helps to ensure that only one solution is possible.

Make Word Trains using suffixes, (–ly, –y, –tion, –er, –ness, –less, and so on). Many roots take multiple suffixes, and so suffix Word Trains are likely to have more than one solution.

Word Train 1 Puzzle Pieces

Copy each Word Train. If possible, use a different color of card stock for each puzzle. Cut out the root-prefix pairs on the thick lines to make 10 pieces per puzzle. All nine words formed in the Word Train puzzle are listed in the *Scholastic First Dictionary*. This page doubles as your answer key.

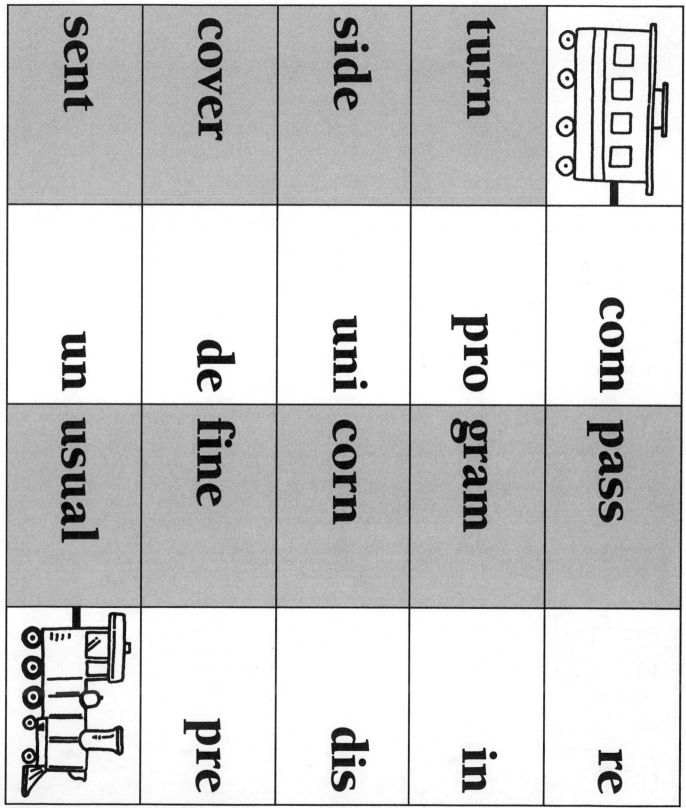

sent	cover	side	turn	
un	de	uni	pro	com
un usual	de fine	uni corn	pro gram	com pass
	pre	dis	in	re

Word Train 2 Puzzle Pieces

Copy each Word Train. If possible, use a different color of card stock for each puzzle. Cut out the root-prefix pairs on the thick lines to make 10 pieces per puzzle. All nine words formed in the Word Train puzzle are listed in the *Scholastic First Dictionary*. This page doubles as your answer key.

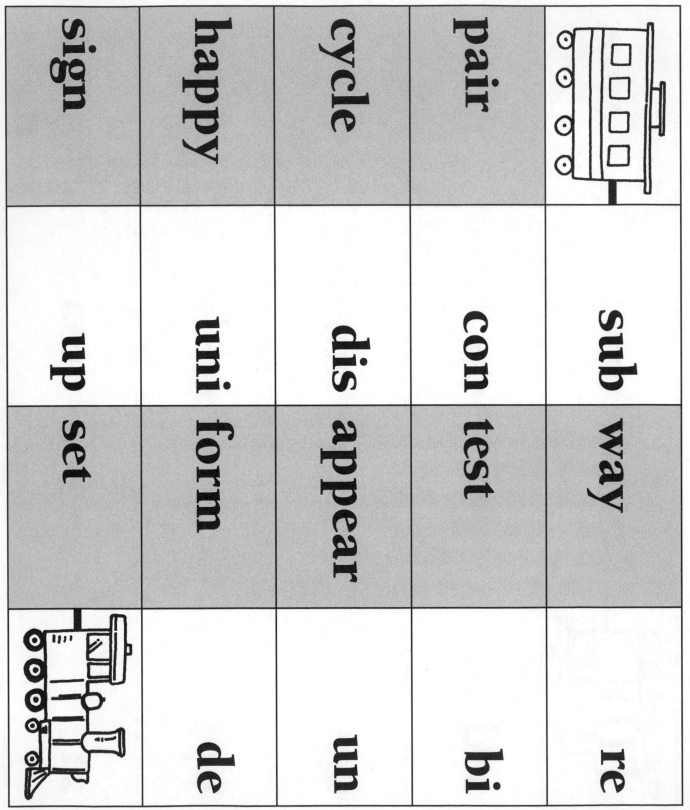

Word Train Template

Use this template to make your own Word Trains. Some additional words in the *Scholastic First Dictionary* include confuse, decide, define, describe, design, except, excite, expensive, explore, inform, inside, invent, invite, present, project, protect, record, relax, repair, remember, return, subtract, underwater, and uniform.

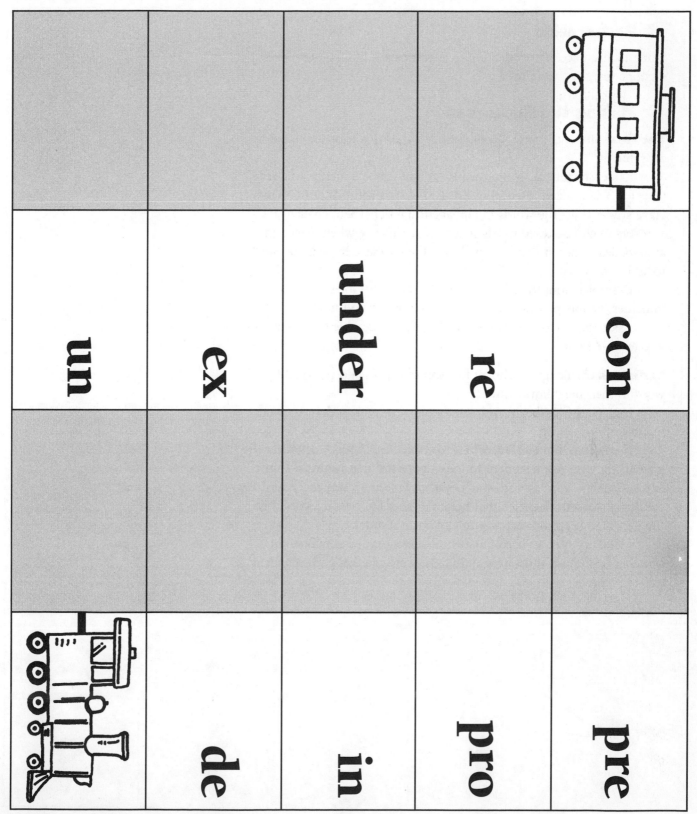

Silly Sentence Safari

Students hunt for dictionary words to make alphabetical sentences.

▶ Preparation

Students need access to a dictionary. If you have a limited number of dictionaries, see "Variations."

▶ Making the Sentences

The Goal Students search for dictionary words that form an alphabetical sentence.

Ask each student to choose a letter and search a dictionary (or a text) for half a dozen interesting words that start with his or her letter. Have students list the words in alphabetical order. Then, challenge students to choose three words that form a sentence when placed in alphabetical order. If they get stuck, tell them to search for more words to add to their list.

Examples from the *Scholastic First Dictionary*: Tables take tall tomatoes. People pet pigs poorly. Neighbors never nod now.

Ask students to illustrate their sentences. Assemble their creations into an A–Z book.

Variations Challenge neighbors to swap sentences and try to add a word to their neighbor's sentence.

Use words that begin with letters in consecutive order: Acrobats bite caterpillars daily.

If you have limited time or few dictionaries, choose a letter for the class to explore. Ask a student to look up a word that begins with the letter. Use that word as a starting point for building a sentence. Students can suggest words that go either before or after the starting word, but the idea is to keep the sentence in alphabetical order.

Make up three to five alphabetical sentences and scramble the sentences. Students must unscramble the words so that each sentence makes sense.

Reproducible Activities

Students use a dictionary to find words in letter puzzles, fill in missing letters, practice using guide words, and pronounce words to complete poems, jokes, rhymes, and riddles.

Word Worm 1 (page 24)

 **Answers**

slime, smile, slide, lime, lime, limes, dime, dimes, slim, sled, sleds, side, meld, melds, mild, dim, dims, elm, elms, die, dies, lie, lies, lid, lids, me, is, id, es, el

Word Worm 2 (page 25)

Answers

stranger, strange, star, stage, sea, sear, set, serge, stag, tag, tan, tar, tang, ran, rat, rag, rage, rang, range, ranger, rate, rater, nag, gnat, gate, gar, great, rear, rest, an, anger, art, at, age, ages, ate, eat, ear, earn, er

Letter Riddle (page 26)

Answers

1. rough 2. octopus 3. poor 4. trash 5. wheel
Riddle: horse

Plural Riddle (page 27)

Answers

1. hobbies 2. teeth 3. heroes 4. wolves 5. kisses
Riddle: stove

Guide Word Poems (pages 28 and 29)

Answers

Poem 1: snail, whale, box, fox
Poem 2: cat, bear, bat, repair

Funny Spelling Rhymes
(pages 30 and 31)

Review the pronunciation guide on page 6 of the *Scholastic First Dictionary*. Encourage students to look up words in the dictionary if they are unsure about spelling.

 **Answers**

Funny Spelling Rhymes 1: 1. coast toast 2. whole bowl 3. high tie 4. mud spud
Bonus: balloon cocoon.

Funny Spelling Rhymes 2: 1. cub club 2. dream team 3. long song 4. mean jeans
Bonus: ocean motion.

Funny Spelling Ha-Has (page 32)

Teachers: Review the pronunciation guide on page 6 of the *Scholastic First Dictionary*. Encourage students to look up words in the dictionary.

Answers

1. What did the second hand say to the minute hand as it passed by? I'll be back in a minute. 2. Why do people at basketball games always stay cool? They're fans. 3. Why won't the alligator eat the clown? Because he tastes a little funny.

Word Worm 1

How many words can you make using these letters?
Use a dictionary to look up words.

lime _____   _____

_____   _____

_____   _____

_____   _____

_____   _____

_____   _____

Word Worm 2

**Start at any letter.
Follow the path
from letter to letter
to make a word.
Example: Follow S to
T to A to R to
make "star."
Use a dictionary
to help you find
lots of words.
Bonus: Find a seven-letter
word that starts with "S."**

star _____ _____

_____ _____

_____ _____

_____ _____

_____ _____

Letter Riddle

Each word is missing one letter. Look up the words in a dictionary and write the missing letters on the blanks. Those letters spell out the answer to this riddle:

Who Am I?

I wear four shoes.

Not pairs, not twos.

They stay on my feet,

Even while I sleep!

Answer: ____ ____ ____ ____ ____

1 eig____t (number)

2 oct____pus (animal with eight arms)

3 poo____ (not rich)

4 goldfi____h (small pet)

5 whe____l (bikes have two of them)

Plural Riddle

Each plural word is missing one letter. Look up the words in a dictionary. Then write the missing letters on the blanks. Those letters spell out the answer to this riddle:

Who Am I?

I never make dough

Yet I bake many sweets.

I never stir pots.

Yet I cook many treats.

Answer: ____ ____ ____ ____ ____

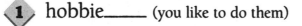

1 hobbie_____ (you like to do them)

2 tee_____h (for chewing)

3 her_____es (brave men)

4 wol_____es (wild animals)

5 kiss_____s (they go with hugs)

Guide Word Poem 1

**Look up each guide
word in the Scholastic
First Dictionary.
Find the other guide
word on the same page.
Write it on the blank.
The first one is done
for you.**

Who Am I?

I'm bigger than a _____ **snail** _____.
(soccer)

I'm smaller than a _____.
(weed)

I fit inside a wooden _____.
(bread)

My name is furry _____.
(friendly)

Guide Word Poem 2

Look up each guide
word in the Scholastic
First Dictionary.
Find the other guide
word on the same page.
Write it on the blank.
The first one is done
for you.

Why Did I Do That?

I like to tickle a _____ _cat_ _____.
(cart)

Don't try to tickle a _____.
(before)

I tried it with a _____.
(bean)

Which then needed _____.
(recorder)

Funny Spelling Rhymes 1

Read the questions. Each answer is a rhyme, like "red bed." But the second word is spelled the way it sounds. Sound out the word. Then write the correct spelling in the blank.

1 What is a scary breakfast?

ghost _____
(tohst)

2 What is a dish that is not broken?

whole _____
(bohl)

3 How do tall people make knots?

tie _____
(hie)

4 What is a dirty potato?

spud _____
(muhd)

Bonus: What does a fat caterpillar become?

balloon _____
(kuk-koon)

Funny Spelling Rhymes 2

Read the questions. Each answer is a rhyme, like "red bed." But the words are spelled the way they sound. Sound out each word. Then write the correct spelling in the blank.

1 Where do baby bears meet?

cub _____
(kluhb)

2 Who are sleepy basketball players?

_____   _____
(dreem)   **(teem)**

3 What tune goes on and on?

_____   _____
(lawng)   **(sawng)**

4 What are tight pants that hurt?

_____   _____
(meen)   **(jeenz)**

Bonus: What makes people seasick?

_____   _____
(oh-shuhn)   **(moh-**shuhn)

Name: _____ Date: _____

Funny Spelling Ha–Has

Read these jokes aloud. Some words are
spelled the way they sound. Sound them out.
You can also look them up in a dictionary.

1 **Funny Joke** (**fuhn**-nee **johk**)

What did the (**sek**-uhnd) hand of a clock say to

the (**lit**-l) hand as it (**past**) (**bie**)?

I'll be (**bak**) in a (**min**-uht).

2 **Funnier Joke** (**fuhn**-nee-uhr **johk**)

Why do (**pee**-puhl) at (**bas**-kit-bahl) (**gaymz**) (**awl**-wayz)

stay (**kool**)?

They're (**fanz**).

3 **Funniest Joke** (**fuhn**-nee-est **johk**)

Why won't the (**al**-uh-gayt-uhr) (**eet**) the (**kloun**)?

Because he (**taysts**) a (**lit**-l) (**fuhn**-ee)!